PLANT FRUITS & SEEDS

David M. Schwartz *is an award-winning author of children's books, on a wide variety of topics, loved by children around the world.* Dwight Kuhn's *scientific expertise and artful eye work together with the camera to capture the awesome wonder of the natural world.*

For a free color catalog describing Gareth Stevens Publishing's list of high-quality books and multimedia programs, call 1-800-542-2595 (USA) or 1-800-461-9120 (Canada). Gareth Stevens Publishing's Fax: (414) 225-0377.

Library of Congress Cataloging-in-Publication Data

Schwartz, David M.
  Plant fruits & seeds / by David M. Schwartz; photographs by Dwight Kuhn.
    p. cm. — (Look once, look again)
  Includes bibliographical references (p. 23) and index.
  Summary: Introduces, in simple text and photographs, the fruits or seeds
of an apple, maple, oak, hemlock, milkweed, corn, and kiwi.
  ISBN 0-8368-2427-X (lib. bdg.)
  1. Seeds—Juvenile literature. 2. Fruit—Juvenile literature. [1. Seeds. 2. Fruit.]
I. Kuhn, Dwight, ill. II. Title. III. Series: Schwartz, David M. Look once, look again.
  QK661.S388   1999
  575.6'8—dc21   99-18607

This North American edition first published in 1999 by
Gareth Stevens Publishing
1555 North RiverCenter Drive, Suite 201
Milwaukee, Wisconsin 53212 USA

First published in the United States in 1998 by Creative Teaching Press, Inc., P.O. Box 6017, Cypress, California, 90630-0017.

Printed in the United States of America

1 2 3 4 5 6 7 8 9 03 02 01 00 99

PLANT

FRUITS & SEEDS

by David M. Schwartz

photographs by Dwight Kuhn

A SPRINGBOARDS INTO
SCIENCE
SERIES

Gareth Stevens Publishing

MILWAUKEE

What tasty fruit has firm, white flesh and a five-pointed star?

5

LOOK AGAIN

When you cut an apple in half,
you can see its star.
An apple's seeds sit in five openings.
They make a star in the apple's core.
Outside the core is the sweet,
delicious part of the apple.
This is the part people
and animals like to eat.

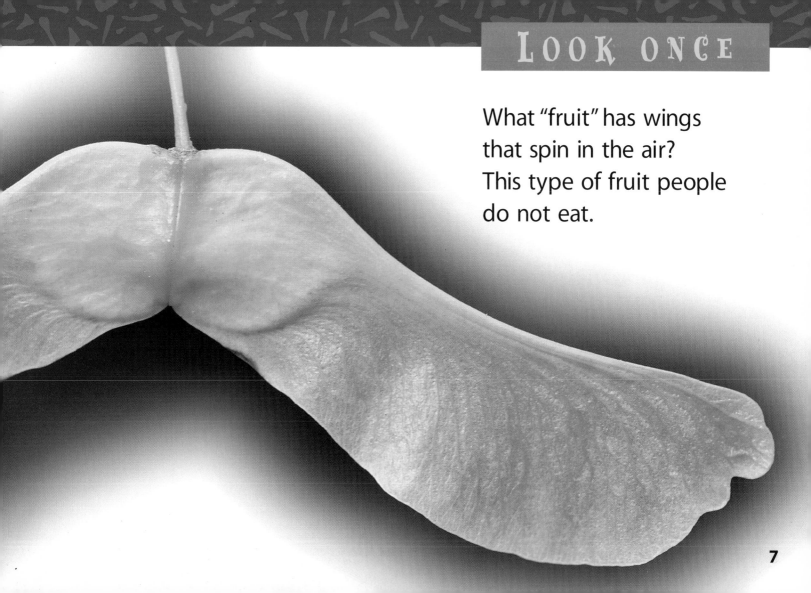

What "fruit" has wings
that spin in the air?
This type of fruit people
do not eat.

The flat, curved fruit
of a maple tree has
two wings. The wings are
joined in the middle.
When the fruit is ripe,
it falls from the tree
and spins to the ground.

Inside each wing is a seed.
In moist earth, the wings rot
and the seeds sprout.
A new maple tree may grow
from any of the seeds.

A mighty tree could
grow from this tiny fruit.

Acorns are the "fruits" of oak trees. One oak tree may have fifty thousand acorns. If an acorn falls on soft earth, the seed inside may grow into a new oak tree. People do not eat this type of "fruit."

This also is a "fruit" that you would not want to eat.

Pinecones are the fruits of evergreen trees. These cones are from a hemlock tree. The cones contain seeds that some birds like to eat.

This seed looks like
a fluffy parachute.
It comes from a plant
with milky sap.

The "fruit" of a milkweed plant is called
a pod. When the pod splits open,
silky fluff bursts out.
Seeds are attached
to the fluff. When
the wind blows, the
fluff carries the seeds
like parachutes. That is
how milkweed seeds
travel to new places.

If the seeds land in soft soil, they
may grow into new milkweed plants.

This plant has ears,
but it cannot hear.

This kind of ear is the
"fruit" of a corn plant.
The ear is wrapped in
a grassy husk.
Peel away the husk
to find rows of kernels.
The kernels are the
seeds of the fruit.

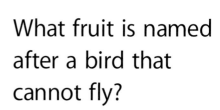

What fruit is named after a bird that cannot fly?

Kiwis are birds that cannot fly. They have a rounded shape and are a little fuzzy. Kiwi fruits are also rounded and fuzzy. They have small, black seeds and pale green flesh.

A.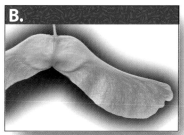

B.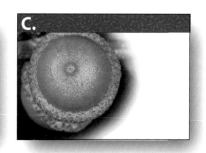

C.

D.

E.

F.

G.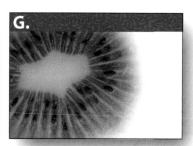

Look closely. Can you name these fruits and seeds?

A. Apple

B. Maple

C. Oak (acorns)

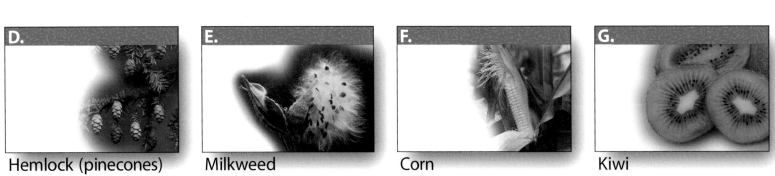

D. Hemlock (pinecones)

E. Milkweed

F. Corn

G. Kiwi

How many were you able to identify correctly?

acorn: the fruit of an oak tree.

core: the center part of something, such as an apple or the Earth.

ear: the part of a grain plant, such as corn, that contains the seeds of the plant.

fruit: the reproductive part of a seed plant.

husk: the dry, outer covering of a seed or nut.

kernel: the seed of a grain plant, such as wheat or corn.

kiwi: a fruit with pale green flesh and black seeds; a bird from New Zealand that cannot fly. Both the fruit and the bird are fuzzy.

moist: wet; damp.

pale: light in color; not dark.

parachute: something that is used to slow the fall of a person or object that is moving through the air. The fluff on a milkweed seed acts like a parachute for the seed.

pinecone: the scaly part of an evergreen tree that contains the seeds of the tree.

pod: the seed case of a plant, such as a bean plant or milkweed plant, that splits open when it is ripe and releases the seeds.

ripe: fully grown and developed, like fruit that is ready to be picked and eaten.

sap: the liquid that flows through a plant carrying food for the plant.

silky: soft and smooth, like silk cloth.

sprout *(v)***:** to produce new growth in a plant.

ACTIVITIES

A is for Apple

Play an alphabet game with a friend or family member. Start with the letter *A*, and think of a fruit (a seed or something with seeds inside) that starts with that letter. Take turns with the other person, trying to get through the alphabet to *Z*. If you need help, visit the produce section of a supermarket, or look for books in the library that show the various kinds of fruits.

Cone Figures

Collect some evergreen pinecones (make sure you have permission to collect the cones), or purchase them in a craft store. Imagine that each cone is the body of a person or animal. Use a variety of materials, such as pipe cleaners, Styrofoam balls, and felt, to add a head, arms, and legs. Add details, such as eyes and a nose, to the figure with markers.

What's Inside?

With an adult's help, cut open different kinds of fruits, such as grapes and apples. How many seeds can you count inside each fruit? Draw a picture of each type of fruit and the seeds inside. You could also dip the cut fruit in paint and stamp designs on construction paper.

Seed Mosaic

Use a variety of dried seeds — such as beans, peas, and lentils — to make a colorful design. Draw a large, simple geometric design or object (triangle or pyramid) on a piece of cardboard. Starting at the center, spread a little white glue on the cardboard, and press seeds of one kind into place. Spread glue on another section, and press seeds of a different type into place. Continue to add glue and seeds until the mosaic is complete.

More Books to Read

All About Seeds. Susan Kuchalla (Troll Associates)

Flowers, Fruits, Seeds. Jerome Wexler (Prentice Hall Books for Young Readers)

From Seed to Plant. Gail Gibbons (Holiday House)

How a Seed Grows. Helene J. Jordan (HarperCollins)

The Nature and Science of Seeds. Exploring the Science of Nature (series).
   Jane Burton and Kim Taylor (Gareth Stevens)

Trees, Leaves, and Bark. Young Naturalist Field Guides (series). Diane L. Burns (Gareth Stevens)

Videos

All About Seeds. (Film Ideas)

A Flowering Plant from Seed to Seed. (International Film Bureau)

What's Inside a Seed? (Coronet, The Multimedia Co.)

Web Sites

tqjunior.advanced.org/3715/seeds4.html

www.alienexplorer.com/ecology/e107.html

Some web sites stay current longer than others. For further web sites, use your search engines to locate the following topics: *apples, fruit, maples, milkweeds, oaks, pinecones, seeds,* and *trees.*

INDEX